CW00751653

Born in Illinois and raise
Jeremy Toombs set out as s
lands such as Seattle, Alaska, South Korea, Thailand,
India, South America, and settled (for now) in the fine
city of Bristol, England not to be confused with Bristol,
Tennessee which he's never been to. Jeremy really likes
chocolate cake with vanilla ice cream. But really, he only
likes his mom's chocolate cake with a particular type of
vanilla ice cream (Schwan's) and anytime he eats any
other cake or ice cream he laments that he's not in his
mom's kitchen.

Ten Thousand Things

Jeremy Toombs

Anthony
I really enjoyed your set.
Thanks. Enjoy these poems.

Peace,

Burning Eye

This edition published by Burning Eye Books 2013

Printed and Bound by Bell and Bain Ltd, Glasgow

www.burningeye.co.uk

@burningeye

Burning Eye Books
15 West Hill, Portishead, BS20 6LG

ISBN 978 1 90913 618 2

www.jeremytoombs.com

CONTENTS

TEN THOUSAND THINGS

Han Shan

I know the songs of purple mushrooms. Eat them.
– Han Shan

It was cold mountain, the poet:
spoken in the wind
held firm enough in stone
grasped momentarily
set about for time no time.

The poem
is set twice:
once in the mind
once to stone
pointing to beyond poetry
to what exists
seen briefly
and set twice:
once in the mind
once to stone.

To Basho

How I wish you could travel now
across this world; you could
have the dust of far continents
to wash off of your sandals:

salmon jumping leaving ripples
moose galloping between tundra lakes
the easy movements of eagles
and swallows diving into cliffs

the heat of a tropical sun
washed away in tropical rains
sunsets sliding down over flat lands
and the stars of the southern hemisphere
just out of sight.

In Japan we could drink sake
writing haikus on mountain narrow trails
and feeling winter, put on the heavy
coats, move to the lowlands.

In a Kentucky oak tree shade
we'd drink bourbon by
a salt lick, watch for white-tail deer
and hear a dog howl.

Li Po
(copied from a painting
by Liang k'ai)

Li Po

descended from Lao Tzu
descended from the Turks
youthful wanderer
enfant terrible   knight errant
drunkard poet

Did you kill several men:
your blade following the way through
the air – swish of sword, rush of wind
the last sounds your victim knows?

rejecter of empire
generals in your blood

curious for curiosity's sake
natural philosopher
child's mind
recognized genius
compassionate and perceptive

Li Po: human follower, existent, one who still lives.

June Bug

Most kids, they pay attention about 80-85% of the time. The rest of the time they're doing kids stuff. Picking their noses, Talking. Writing on the table. Picking on each other. But for the occasional child, that behavior percentage is reversed. So it was for June-affectionately called June-Bug by me. June Bug was always doing his own thing.

Do your thing June Bug!
Erratic flight of mind
manic joyous being of light and smile
I want to comprehend this world as you.
And I apologize for all the yelling, all the pushing you
to conform to the arbitrary rules of a foreign tongue
with you so young and so fresh and with the tiger's power.
What good is English for you, oh child bodhisattva of light and smile?

Anyway, the rules, such as they were,
were always loose upon your feet
for you to kick off at will.

I have great hopes for you, June Bug,
that you will grow up
and still be a saint.

The New (the old)
The Tai Chi sequence

Close and far
together;
there is no thing without
the other.
there are
ten thousand things.

Drawing silk
painting a wall
swimming with the dragon:
these things should be done
but with great care.

Daily
we look
closely, minutely
at the natural
at the self,
all the while
discovering the new (the old).

I have come better
to know my body:
this mass of muscle,
body of bone, tendons,
organs, fat –
held together by the same
energy
that ignited the sun.

The New (the old)
The Chi Sequence

15

Immortality Blues

How many lifetimes
spirits
reincarnations
meditation hardships
nights, days
wanderings
selfless good deeds
how much self-inflicted harm
how many prayers
magic tricks
beggar's meals
rain soaked days, nights
sun burnt bodies
bruised feet
mountains climbed

Oh, how many times in all of the world
and all of these lives shall I close these eyes
or those past eyes, or eyes to come, only to open
them again to another day?

Buddhist Monks Don't

Buddhist monks don't do certain things.
We all know they don't
eat meat
smoke
drink beer or whiskey
or have pretty young wives.

But they also don't lie in late
under warm down duvets
reading about oneness

instead of practicing.

Buddhist Monks don't...

Cambodia

We rode by on motorbikes;
the red dust covering our backs
and the people we passed
either they looked up or
they did not look up.

Daily existence removed
200 years except for the
village tractor and a few motorbikes.

The lives of Cambodians
outside of cities, the country
people: smiling, surviving.

It was these people a millennia
ago carrying stones, carving stones
worshipping what the stones represented.

It was these people 25 years ago
herded and gathered
torn apart and thrown in heaps.

It is these people now
still kneeled in prayer hands together
or wading in the fields of rice

and those were smiling who looked up.

Cheong Ek Genocidal Center

A place of cattle grazing
and chickens pecking in
the excavated graves

fragments of clothes
impressed into the ground

worn dirt walkways
meander around craters

The Khmer Rouge: no respecter
of persons; all sorts have died here.
The bones still lie about.

Ta Prohm

Trees crawl down through
buildings, roots down through stone;
a symbiotic coupling
like flesh and bone.

There is too much age here
to comprehend.
Who knows of the beginning?
Who can see the end?

Where man has laid down treasure
nature has brought down ruin.

Only birds, butterflies, and lizards
live here as far as I see; lots of insects, perhaps some snakes.
I do know this: the kings and priests, they've been gone.

Pre-dawn Bangkok

Taxicab ride up on the elevated highway
the red warning lights on high rises
make up
the cityscape like some crazy cosmos
of hieroglyphic constellations.
        The imagination fills in the scene: a dragon,
a bullock drawn wagon, a girl carrying water, a god glancing back
over his right shoulder, the blinking red eyes of a demon, a raised
staff, a coiled serpent and the sky now showing some light and me
leaving town for home.

Electric Light Buddha Altar / 2:20am Hua Hin Station

The bell rings two times.
Our train sits.
It is peaceful.
The touts have gone home to sleep.
No water or rice for sale.

The train engine starts slowly
pulling the cars down the track;
momentum now gaining.
The train passing by
a long unused volleyball court
dark urban ruins
sleeping houses
big silent buildings
red light tipped radio towers
and in someone's back yard
an electric light Buddha altar.

6:01 Bam Bamru

Six or seven or eight passengers disembark.
The train, as always, is tentative about moving again
as if it would like to stay awhile, perhaps to rest.

But trains, they need no rest;
not these steel beasts
coursing up the Thai peninsula
and barely glancing
to the east through the coconut tree screen
to see the sky
slowly turning its morning colors: sable to
blush to bluish white blue tinged with pink, the day dawning on.

The corrugated tin-roofed shanties
lining some parts of the rail
then impenetrable railroadside vegetation
and then what I think is Bangkok
slowly pulls itself into my view.

We cross a river. There's a junk, a barge, a longboat, a house on stilts,
and our train crossing on a bridge.

Fuji-San

From this aeroplane window
Fuji-San sits on the clouds.

Ever so often I see
smaller ranges
snow covered.

Snow white whiter
          than cloud white.

When one sees Fuji-San
it is impossible to think
that it is anything else.

Mountain Spirit holds sway over
land and sea and air
as far as the eye can see.

Looks like an easy climb: right up the side slope
come slidin' down the other
land in the clouded bottom.

What if it blew it's top?
Right now?

Chopsticks

forceful pinch crosses
sticks, kimchi drops down bowlside
chopsticks like the breeze:
or rolling a cigarette:
tender paper, easy tear

Chopsticks

Soju

sitting Korean
curbside, contemplating my
hangover, eating
pringles, drinking a coke
and maybe buying a cat.

Nankai Station

I feel stares on my head;
glancing up,
faces avert.
In exiting,
rising Corinthian columns
stacked on Japanese tile mosaics

The Toyo Hotel

The Toyo washroom
toilet water for my ass
oh, it feels so good!

IT HAPPENED IN INDIA

Temple Morning

There are lions and gods
on the temple facade:
multi-tiered multi-colored
multiple figures locked in meditation
or in positions of praise.
Gods and holy men giving hand mudra blessings.

Round and round inside the wall, around the inner sanctum I see
a cow, a man in a light blue lungi, man in a white lungi,
woman in a narrow gold trimmed sari, yellow sari...

There's a lot of people this temple morning just walkin'
around and around
somewhere in there there's the temple elephant what took
twenty rupees from me yesterday
and blessed my head
with an elephant kiss.

Temple Night

The last night for the sight
of the Vishnu Temple to catch
my eyes with its golden top
perched on a blue and red dome
with its sides the home of lions
and gods. They are looking out over
Madurai as I am looking out over
Madurai. And I, I am as much a lion,
or as much a god, as these.

Monkey

Monkeys at the temples!
Monkeys in the temples!
Monkeys on the temples!
Big Monkeys
Little Monkeys
Mama Monkeys
Baby Monkeys
Big Bad Daddy Monkeys
A hundred Monkeys all over the temples
and our train just rolls on by.

Oh, the bouldered fields of Hampi
out on the rocks, the boulders of Hampi,
huge boulders piled up
climbing up the bouldered hills
I see a sentinel monkey sitting
boulder perched, non-moving.

Monkeys all around looking around,
chilling.
Some Monkeys taking it in, some Monkeys making it.
Some Monkeys can sit in one place, so long
just sitting
for a long, long time.

They get a bad rap, Monkeys, for having rajasic minds
moving around all the time.
But it ain't true. I say it ain't.
Now, I ain't no wildlife biologist or zoologist or anything,
but I see that Monkey ain't moved in a long while.
Just sitting. Chilling.
I bet that Monkey
ain't thinking about nothing.
Meditating.
Monkey.
Monk.
Monk Monkey.
I'm just jealous
they got them long tails.

Monkey

Dragonfly

red red dragonflies
make love
dart about
with the trees and sky above
reflected in the backdrop stream

water spiders
little fishes and tadpoles
cavort

water plants rooted in water
float slowly
or just float because

it's too hot to move
for me it's too hot to stay

Rain Sequence: Storm in Rishikesh

great jagged forked strike of lightning
down behind yonder mountain
          some piece of ground got fried
I suppose some sadhus are sitting
sheltered in safe caves.

Oh, great fury of the skies: windblown mists amidst the peaks
rain falling;
cars creeping up the mountain look small and slow and quiet.

If I went up the mountain
right now
into the clouds of smoke and fire,
would god speak to me?
Strike me down?
Or, would I just get wet?

Oh, how the rain falls!
          Will I get wet going for dosa?
I think: yes.

Yogi blues chant
shrute box drone
yogi blues wail
rain fall rhythm on the roof
thunder in the valley
pen scratch on paper
wind
and one thousand other things that perhaps only dogs can hear.

light rain
drops.
light rain
drops hang.
light rain
drops hang off of leaves.
some fall.
new
light rain
drops form.

Storm in Rishkesh

Rust (a process)

rust colored red railway station roadside rain water
rust colored
    railway side rainwater
        from the red rocks
           red rocks
              red rocks southern red clay rocks

The rainwater puddles of rust colored rainwater
rust colored puddles
the red dirt wet red mud

rust colored rain water puddles
      beside the railway station

Monsoon rain season turns India green
turns rainwater puddles red
turns my skin and hair wet
clothes wet rocks wet
rainwater shroud falling down mountain side
    fills up rivers filling up
rainwater rushing over rocks
rain even comes down in my train
bags are wet with rain
rain rain it rains
all is wet wet
the clouds just sit
wet like red rust colored railroadside rainwater puddles

Buffalo

Buffalo could be religion.
I'm searching at night
looking for eyes red in the light.
Searching, looking, not seeing.
But I believe
Buffalo is nearby here
although I can only hear frogs
crickets
cars far off
me talking.

I see the moon unseen
bright right through cloud cover,
clouds very low,
starry sky very high
with Venus shining.

Ancients knew of the sky goddess,
grew out of it,
and here I am,
looking for Buffalo.

Ganesh Blues
for Blue Ganesh

How's it feel to be forgotten, Blue Ganesh?
Your home under rock boulder jumble cave
sand colored rocks marked with colored rust red bands
green rocks and white stripes.
I can see light coming down
but can't see the sky with your boulder home
obscuring my view.
What I can see is you,
Sri Ganesh colored Blue
   two white eyes kum kum bindi
   painted Blue Ganesh on painted red stone
   sitting alone next to a broken off yoni
   a jolly old fella with a big Blue belly

Little Blue temple Ganesh
Blue cave temple Ganesh
Blue Blue cave temple Ganesh
Blue Blue Ganesh

HP Gas Void

A short path beyond
all meaning removed, ego gone,
no answers, no questions in mind,
no mind.

Only void all void
and void realized fills up
with terror of Nothing
and not ready for it at all
and scared. Shitless.

Shit is everywhere,
on my leg, on my lungi,
on the porch by the gate
in a big round patty.

My mind is not ready for dissolution of ego
I am wild, animalistic, squatting in the flower garden naked
wary of people and then ashamed, in my Adam-mind, of nudity;
hiding behind walls
then crawling on the ground, a sarong half on
and not even able to cry out for help.

Too weak.
Can't move.
Can't think.
Only feel bad, real bad.
Oh, how bad it feels,
when Nothing
is going on.

Ki Jai

Mahatma Gandhi ki jai
      Dr. King ki jai
Mahatma Gandhi ki jai
      Dr. King ki jai
Victory to Gandhi-ji
Victory to Dr. King
Victory to Truth
Victory to Peace
Peace is the truth through
      which we can be free.
Victory to non-violent resistance.
For it's the truth that will liberate your existence from this illusion of
      confinement.
See how the empire was bent when Gandhi-ji walked
down to the sea for a handful of salt
with no fear nor dread
with ten-thousand at his back he tread:
Gandhi-ji was the proof the British could see
Gandhi-ji was the truth and India became free.

Hear now how Dr. King asked the people of Alabama to take to their
      feet
when Rosa Parks refused to move; yea, she kept her seat
in the face of southern white hellions
she held her ground and went to jail and
Dr. King said hear me now people:
Take to the streets, move those feet or car pool
ride a horse or ride a mule or ride a bike
wear out them shoes, get them old walking blues,
but don't take the bus.
Do this for your children for their trust is in us.

Let us look now to the youth to see how they run: they have no fear
      as they are tuned to sound of Om.
All children live in a world called home where peace and truth are
      known as one.
Thus is the essence of Dr. King's dream: to escape how this world
      seems to us.

So boycott the bus
> or walk to the sea.

Listen to Dr. King.
Follow Gandhi-ji.
Peace will bring the victory.
Truth will show the way.
Let us point our feet to the kingdom to come.
Let's start the march today.

Allepey Express

An early morning exodus on the Allepey Express to Ernakalum and the 7:00am orange orb sun turns to dawn gray to pink as the train picks up speed.
It's not over the treetops yet, the sun.
The last one of 2007 to shine on this earth with its 72,000 channels of solar energy feeding the 72,000 energy channels of this muscle and blood, flesh and bone, mind and spirit of human existence which is nothing more than the same existence as a tree or a rock which is also the same thing as the culmination of the thousands of moments (one moment) of the existence of reality.

I seek to find and lose myself at this moment in meditation as my physical composition loses its edges and the individual particles and waves of me are set free to float to the highest levels of Earth's atmosphere and even beyond to Mars, Jupiter, Saturn, Andromeda, Tatooine, and then solidifying once again in the thousandth incarnation of spirit; this time as a jawa roaming throughout the desert in a massive sand crawler scouring for droids to steal, buy, barter, sell, destroy and repair; turning circuits and microchips and data processors and programs into semi-conscious beings of metal and electricity with reasoning ability and some able to translate even the arcane language of moisture evaporators as well as 6 million other forms of communication both organic and inorganic.

It's these non-human mechanics of the mind
that keep us bound to time
tryin' to keep up keeps us out of line
and searching
searching too hard
makes our true peace hard
too hard to find.
That's why I'm ridin' this
Allepey Express to a destination;
pullin' into a station: Where are we?
What's the name of this place?
I can't see the sign.

Allepey Express

MADE IN ENGLAND

Irenwe ha

Initially
   it was this soil this air this water
this soil that made my bones
   fed into me
this air that made my spirit
   flew into me
this water that made my blood
   flooded into me.

I am he that speaks the regular way.
I am returned to the beginning.
I am the roots deep in soil drawing water
  the leaves pulling in sun.
I left to come back in several different ways.

I am spread open now reaching
stuck in Alaska mud flats
lazing in Kentucky heat
running up and down Bukhan-san
astounded on the sub-continent
revelling in Leigh Woods, Stokes Croft
mistaken for a Texan
mistaken for a Tennessean
in Koh Phangan controlling galaxies
but that first inhalation, in Irenwe ha
my bloods first run, Ilinwe k.
My bones made in Illinois.

The Riot Suite
from The Arts House Window

Summertime
    and the streets are burning
      coppers are standing
        shoulder to shoulder in line
    they say that Tesco's burning
      but this world keeps on turning
so hush now people, there's no sleep tonight

Rosy's street dancing
playing saxophone Summertime
Fire's burning turning the night sky
      blacker with smoke
helicopter searchlight
      shinin' through
What are people gonna do?
       heartbeats jacked
       bottles smacked against concrete

Stokes Croft folks still movin' their feet
shoutin' out:
  Our streets   whose streets?
    Our streets whose streets?
      Our streets
bangin' on plastic bins
the feelin's movin' in
     to my bones
police lines advance
     the mob runnin' in retreat
What's the chance this is over any time soon?

I wish the searchlights were the moon.
I wish the police were trees.
I wish people throwin' bottles would turn to peace.

It's your town you've lit on fire.
Don't you see they've conspired for this to be?

Let us sing out instead: Om Namo Narayana Om Namo Narayana
Om Namo Narayana

These fires can't be put out;
they'll burn through the summer,
the stench of plastic
thick.
These things stick: glass breakin', fire burnin', K-9 dogs, cops advancin',
People hiding their faces.
But this place is safe, a haven.
I wonder now where Rosy's gone to.

****

Now I hear:
the sweeping of brooms
helicopter spotlight showing the clean-up
battered police vans convoy by
their leaving cheered
glass crunching under the tires.
My heart beat
is still pounding
beating to the rhythm
of helicopter blades.

****

Three days later
I see fire flames flashing
        out the window
jumping up thinking 'fire!'
feeling the fear
and seeing it's only tail lights
stopping, an indicator flashing.

there's still something crashing
        inside, fighting for space
going into the same silence
non-moving I knew
three nights past

feeling the windows vibrate under my fingertips
flames flashing in my peripheral vision
police vans sounding out
blue lights and sirens.

I don't even know now: was I
feeling the lights
seeing the glass break
tasting the air
my sensory recall is shot no thought just takin' it in
and takin' it in.

I do know my heart was beating breaking
for this evidence tells me
there are some folks
that are not trying
to get along
their faces covered by riot masks
covered by balaclava
hiding their better natures.

Three days later
        I'm still shaken
thinking break lights are fires.

****

Now the riot memory settles
    sadly
the residue leaving me blue
when I find myself in contemplation
the flow of thought caught up in sorrow
heaviness, a depression.

It's now evident
when needs go unmet, unheard
people turn to absurdity, to violence.

I will go against this.

Hangover Meatbelly

Hangover
Meatbelly
Legit reasons to quit
going uphill hurts my head
and my gut sticks out
with Meatbelly.

My brain is bashing itself against my skull.
My body weakened by Hangover
being wrought by bourbon aged four years in charred oak barrels
after being distilled with Kentucky spring water through copper
stills then to the bottle, over the ice, in the glass, in the hand, in the
mouth, savoured, swallowed and distilled again into the blood.

Also-Meatbelly
brought about by putting dead animals in my belly after them being
killed, cut apart, chopped up, plastic wrapped, shipped to Bishopton
Sainsbury's, put on offer, bought, fried and eaten by me.

And now it's Hangover Meatbelly
a compound malady incapacitating me today
done in by my own hand:
Hangover Meatbelly
Hangover Meatbelly.

Gone and Unknown

Long these steps spiralling
have been tread
by men long centuries dead.
Who were they? The bells tolled by whom?
Who quick stepped across
the beam spanned o'er the roof
through to another door and to where?
For what?

And higher still
are the bell tower heights
with wind blown hard
and a view of Bristol
centuries old and new; who
came here to look? For why?

One can see pinnacle to pinnacle
St. Mary Redcliffe to St. Nicks
Totterdown to Clifton Row.
A history in church towers and architecture, some slave built
and many, many surely killed
the floors filled in with their bones
and the Bible tome no defense
for the meek only inherit the earth by death, dying,
being buried, decomposing back into the soil
but their toil still evident these days;
unappreciated by those with wealth enough to be vaulted in crypts
their names scripted in marble like it means anything
that I know what their bones are called.

I'd rather know those nameless bones
those hands that built, those feet that tread
and when I am dead bury me not, don't scribe my name in marble
but bathe me in the fire
take me to that tower high
let my burnt up bones blow on Bristol
catch up in air currents
settle somewhere nobody knows

for my sympathy lies there among those others unknown
their hands that worked, their feet that tread down the years
        unappreciated
but their efforts still tangible and smooth
beneath my hands.

Cleopatra

Thatch-roofed eaves
do still drip down as the sun
does now shine while fair
agonizing Cleopatra
does burn with furious passion
at such honest bad news.
Those Nile born blues a kingdom
she would surely pay to lose.

Instead, her currency flows
in tears and writhing and murderous shrieks
and abuse wrongly heaped
upon the head of the messenger.

The lesser part of her debased
and her face does run to Rome
where Mark Antony does join with Octavia.

As course does lead onto course,
the asp bites.
        Grief now is peace.

Darby Garden Meadow Massacre

October 28th 3pm, Darby Garden, Chapel Green Lane, Redland,
Bristol.

It's a sad say in the Darby garden as a day full of sunshine has led to
full scale slaughter:
A ferocious uncaring metal bladed machine mowed down the mad
meadow, home to a little frog seen hopping away crying, his home
destroyed, done in.

A disaster. And who's the master of this mayhem?
Well, I did wield the mad mowing machine
what masticated the meadow
but I was just doing what I was told.
Is that an excuse?
Will the grass forgive?
I don't know. I'll just take my money, get some whiskey,
and not think about the senseless slaughter of the unhappy hopping
frog's home
not think about how morning dew is grass tears
or how the trees are watching
waiting for a chance to drop a branch on my head.

No, I'll not think about it.
Just give me my money, man.
I'll buy some whiskey
and not think about it.

Darby Garden Fox

City fox, it's you
I see eye to eye
looking the worse for wear.

You pause   only brief enough to not be moving
and gone
off down behind the annex
through the fence.

Do you know that that longing in your blood
is for the woodlands, the fields you miss
or have you grown into the city
like we have
and all looking the worse for wear.

Darby Garden Fox

JAZZ, BLUES

To BJ

sweet soul saxophone sounding out loudly
finger pads pounding out rhythms pulsing
all the way back to Miles, Coltrane, Sonny
play for us eternal – we can all feel you.

In the upper aisles a red beard sage dances
just like 42nd street hipsters – dance
just like those Christmas slave holidays – dance
that mother Africa eternal – dance.

I wanted to wile out but just tapped feet
betraying my soul, feeling I was old
afraid of the inside me I might meet
and thinking maybe it's not really cool.

Now I relate how my friend was dancing
beautiful, free and I chained to my chair.

To Kerouac

I've tried it all Kerouac: read
your Dharma, tried to use the wine
bottle, tried to close emotion
down to suppress the suffering.

Now it's 4 am morning toss-
ing, pissed off can't sleep blues; drowning-
liquor even bringing restless
rising heartbright thought empty.

Here the main rub: jealousy down
deep, unrealized until seeing
her dancing and I drunken, falling down stairs. What to do now, Jack?

Jazz Night

rain puddle streetlight shine
night-time soul man breathing
lifelines pulsating
a wall of sound pushing behind the blues
drum beats driving

people all around picking up pieces
love loss hits so hard so hard
falling face first
what's the worst way:
death or slow jazz juke joints?

On Seeing My Looped Telephone Cord Move

just hung up and now watching
watching the stretched out telephone cord
constricting, lessening elasticity
moving the cord but not smoothly like breathing, but
spasmodically, creeping and jerking small movements towards
flaccid.

I'm watching wondering when the
power of friction from my apartment's vinyl wood patterned floor
will provide enough resistance to end the
creeping lessening elasticity.
I'm watching wondering about
the end of movement.

Sunday Afternoon

ain't nothin' like a Sunday afternoon
sadness: alone and jazz listenin'
the glistenin' of the kitchen light on a
full glass of alcohol blues; thinkin'
of Kerouac and the lives of the poets:
all that solitude.

absent is the pleasure in turning and saying,
see, look at this,
and sharing the transport of a
song, a scene that turns and turns
upon the soul and hearing a voice mellow
and pacific answering back.

but this is not mine, not for me now. only
a cigarette, a drink,
the contemplation of a moment
when nothing is happening, a solitary freedom
to feel the blood in the fingertips
turning round heading back to the heart.

Sunset in Montevideo

smokestack fire burnin'
in the industrial section
just over the horizon
and getting brighter with
a city sky haze backdrop
and westward ho: lo, I
see the sunset reflection
golden road over the sea
leading my eyes to the pink
undersides of clouds
steady and sedate
movin' over the sea (and that is
where I want to be) and
two boats motor by sounding
strong and also the sounding
of the waves on this sea wall
and a fisherman's reel
spinnin'
and these Rebecca Blues in my head.
later, a street banner: "Porque la vivienda es una prioridad para la gente."
translation: because living is the one priority for the people

Mother Earth Blues

Listen: I bring you the words from Earth.
Singing: Ai~ai~ai~ai
            Ai~ai~ai~ai
                       Ai~ai~ai~ai~~oh~oh~oh
Mother Earth she moans and turns and yells
and burns in the middle
and she cries and she laughs as she cuts
a path through the universe in elliptical orbit
around the sun on the end of the spiral arm
of the Milky Way Galaxy that's in the middle
of a universe that we can't even comprehend.
And Mother Earth, she sings: Ai~ai~ai~ai
                           Ai~ai~ai~ai
                                Ai~ai~ai~ai~~oh~oh~oh
And the sound of the singing reverberates, bouncing off of the outer-
reaches of the atmosphere and plunging slowly to the depths of the
oceans
stirring the emotions of blue whales and giant squids and felt by
kids on every continent
and passing through our bodies and sounding like:
Ohmmm Ohmmmm Ohmmmm

Listen: These are the words from Earth.
        These are the words from Earth.

Sunset Prose
(for Leslie)

11 am walk to my hilltop point to gaze backwards from where I came seeing tundra lakes like the footsteps of a giant playing hop-scotch; also seeing far away blue to gray horizon of hills changing to golden orange clash on blue sea. I see sunset reflections like lined up oranges. wish you were here to see and listen, listening, listen! cliff swallows song and seagull squawks and receding tide rolling gentle and gentler oceanblue breeze cool on hands as writing outside. sun now gentle burst in last bright flare: a goodbye flash with promises of dawn clear and pink and magnificent to behold and smell air fragrance fresh and clean. flowers now spurting and shouting the sundown blues is blues the wanting you here blues the light bright baby blue skytophalf deep down blues water blue all blue with sunset pink sky/sea icing (get it for your next party) perfect moments are to be recognized during occurrence not in construction (Sartre is wrong) perfect moments make life a joy forever like writing from rockseat the sundown blues (thinking of you)/hearing your voice in my head.

Bad Ass Bop

Something fresh still blowin' known as Be-bop.
The high-hat cymbal is crazy mad; the drummers bad.
Everybody's foot-stompin', clappin', tappin' toes; they be
lovin' those boys
on trumpets and saxophones blowin'
crazy, bass players fingers' bangin',

the drum sticks bangin'.
Dizzy 'n' Bird definin' Bop
with improvizised blowin'
knowin' they bad
showin' the new boys
how to be.

To be or not to be.
The beat of Be-Bop bangin'
boys.
Bop
Bad.
And all the people are blowin'
and bowin' down to Freddie Freeloader blowin'
low. Miles and Monk be
bad
with rim shots shootin', bangin'
folks in the head with Bop.
These boys

knockin' folks dead. These boys
don't stop blowin'
Bop.
They be
bangin'
bad.

Bad
boys
bangin'
blowin'

Be-
Bop.
Bad blowin'
boys be
bangin' Bop.

the beat
the beat
the be-bop pop
the beat don't stop
poppin' hands on knees bangin' fingers on keys
blues man blowin' like a hurricane breeze

Peace
be like, you know,
front porch free flows:

smokin'
jokin'
tokens of experience being passed around
in rhyme in time to the sound
of the beat
the beat
the be-bop pop
the beat don't stop
poppin' hand on knees bangin' fingers on keys
blues man blowin' like a hurricane breeze

undercurrents rise up mellow gold tones
jazz-induced highs bringin' us round home
along the way
finger painted trees sway
in lightening flashes
foot stomp flashes

chorus or rain drops fallin' on the road
machine gun rain drops fallin' on the road

rest easy with a heavy load
there's jazz on the road
stories untold
the tunes unfold
the be-bop pop
the beat don't stop
the beat don't the beat don't the beat don't
stop.

Jeremy's Blues

I

Cuttin' through the city
in the mornin',
through the city on the iron vein.

The moon is waning through the window.
The sky is morning blue and plain.

The city lights streak fast by,
a streak of yellow in my eye.

All the passengers are tired.
We all arose before the dawn.
It's such unnatural living to be moving so fast along.

All of a sudden we're in the country:
green hills all around,
waterways and farm fields.

How did we ever come to live in
fast-paced, city-ill towns?

Even now in the country
all the houses look the same.
Tryin' to be like the city
but goin' by another name.

II

Listenin' close to the engine and the whisper of steel wheels on
rails....
I think we're slowing down to a station for pickin' up country people
in a country town.

My body pulls against the stopping;
now moving again,
speeding up through the country.

It's only the distances I can hold still.
Still. Everything is in motion and
pushing hard against the ground.
Even clouds up above in the sky
some days just fall down.

Fog lies down in the valleys.
The dawnin' sun reflects on a lake.
I stare at the sun 'till it's to much for my eyes to take.

III

Seventy-two thousand channels
burn burn burn
explosion and fusion
such violence gives way to life
starts to burn away the fog
starts to burn away the fat
burns away the confusion
by fusing in facts

It gets hotter in the summer wherever you go.
It's so hard to build an igloo when there ain't no snow.
Up in the north the sun's out all night.
When there ain't no darkness things don't sit just right
fit too tight:
walkin' home in the evenin' and it's still light of day.

When you can see so much
you can lose the balance
that comes from knowing
that the sun is, in fact,
always alight.

IV

Balance of memory good and memory bad
Balance of time?
The past has been had.
Balance of increase
Balance of decline
Maya hangs in the balance
like a white gloved mime
making motions in the air
pulling on ropes and trapped
in boxes when nothing's there.

Such an illusion
confusion brings.
Synapses fire backwards
while faeries sing.

A lost world is something
nobody can find.
Only rings in trees can show true time.
No things are with no mind.
Trains run on parallel lines.
I'm going down to Busan; but I ain't ridin' the blinds.

V

Not ridin' the blinds
No I ain't ridin' the blinds
Trains on the track,
My woman's on my mind.
Music written on the hillside that I can't read,
but those steel wheel's singin' sure suits my needs.

Going down to Busan on the iron steed.
The KTX got so much speed.

My train number reads one oh one.
The only things changing are under the sun.
Nothing gets finished before it's done.
Even if the sun burns out,
how will we know?
eight minutes from now could be the end of the show.

VI

Beetle boats movin' out high on the water;
slow moving going through port.

Big ol' Maersk Cargo ship;
I've seen that name before.
This one here in Busan hails from Singapore.

Ships being built sit in skeleton steel constructs that would surely
sink today.
They'll float sometime.

Busan city sits all around the harbour.
High rises risin' up the hill
Somebody up there must be watchin' this boat whose engine throbs
under my ass and into my belly as we pass over the fishes, and we
lock s-foils into attack position and lo and behold we've left the land
behind.

VII

Blue Blue Blue Blue Blue
Blue Blue-green Ocean
Blue Blue Blue Blue
Blue Blue-white sky

Look back to the land there's a lighthouse.
Look up ahead there's the sea.
Look to seat 33 J.
Look there to see me.

I'm going to Japan for a minute.
I'll be back in Seoul tonight.
Boats movin' out on the ocean leave behind a wake of white.
White-blue sky and the white boats
blue-white sky and these blue notes.

VIII

Deep is the ocean.
Deep color blue.
What moves below us,
I cannot fathom.
Out on the horizon there is land (island)
Island: is land
Island is land.
Two sea birds skim waves
feet dip
food to the beak.
I see one try to lift styrofoam.
She then flies on to the horizon, her eyes on the water.
She wants some fish, not styrofoam.
I wonder will I have time for sushi.

IX

Lo and Behold
The bold serrated outline of mountain island.
We go through a swath of green green water.
Here comes Japan.
Here we come, man!
Sun's rise, samurai swords and sushi.
One time world beater
One time atomic wasteland
Zen blues
and the haiku muse.
Jellyfish glow in the ocean.
The ocean gives way to the land.
I don't feel any particular emotion as we glide on into Japan,
just glide on into Japan.

X

Fukuoka is turning into view.
A golden dome reflects the sun.
A spire stands true.
The city lines the sea.
There's a ferris wheel too.

Blue is the color of my pen.
Blue is the color of the water.
Blue is the color of the mountains.
Blue is the color of sky.

Coming into the harbour, I see
boats are going out to sea.
I'd like to go up in yonder mountains the better this ocean to see.

XI

Tochoji Temple
Big Wooden Buddha with Blessing Hands
After viewing ten levels of hell: Buddha demons grey-skinned and
        horned
torturing souls with distended bellys, or maybe those were depictions
        of life.

I walk through the darkness complete that lies under the Buddha, my
hands feeling the carpeted close sinuous snaking hallway. I am safe
here, in the dark, under the Buddha.
I am disappointed to step back into the light, to be able to see again.
The darkness beneath the Buddha
drove the suffering from my sight
now I am
back into the world
back into the light I am.
Soham.

CONDITIONS

Momentary

How are moments defined?
Shapes:
two dimensions of the printed page
three dimensions of the physical existence
infinite limits of rotating sine curves
forming solids about the axes;
on any given point a touch as slight as a breath (a tangent}
able to throw sine curves to cosine curves.
Everything changes to colors.

Colors:
reds yellows blues
only refractions.
In the absence of light the colors are black.

Reds do not exist in darkness.
Yellows do not exist in darkness.
Blues do not exist in darkness.
Darkness does not exist here.
Always, some light slips in even into
closed eyes.

How are moments defined?
shapes and colors: the composition of the physical;
all mutable illusions:
the tangent, the refraction,
a breaking blade of grass,
the instant smoke dissipates or when the last drop falls.
Which to grasp: the last touch or
the next?

Emotion

Emotion: slipknot around intellect
choking out reason with a serpentine
grip, overruling thought like heartbright wrecked
and peacerest disturbed. Walking under lines
of negativity; wallowing pride
unable to follow nature's soft side.

But emotion also like muskodine:
smooth, strong; approaching limits of perfect
moments recognized in the current time
live like running currents of soft setting
pure sunshine flowing down mountain side streams
on up out of blue stronger than daydreams.

Ultimately: pure, complex, unable
to be understood; and never tabled.

The Guts

who knew
       that it's the guts is where it's at?

that pre-natal devotion transferred
and set in motion a sequence of happenings
that leads me to deconstruct
personal emotional mythologies
while down below, the surf is grey and powerful
today.

       today it is the washing,
the cleansing tide
       wind pushed waves
purging the guts

the guts. who knew: that it's the guts is where it's at?

that first umbilical feeding
       gut to gut
just left me hungry

I'm still searching for sustenance.
What's left? Where to look? Where's it at?
You already know: it's in the guts.

Bound

Where are these binds?
        So long bound
they are hard to find and grown into the bones.

There's binds for sinners
        and there's binds for saints.
There's binds for those that is,
binds for those that ain't.

We are all of us bound,
bound to seek things to keep the mind reeling.

I am bound.
Bound to a personal
mythology that quietly says,
 'Go. Do.'

So I go.
So I do.

Made Strong

We made strong.

Made strong of mind to wonder.
Made strong of foot to wander.
Made strong of spirit to blunder.
Made strong of heart so that we can be
strong at heart.

We are made strong enough
to look past the horror, the horror
to see that fear is temporary
that love is always left.

Made strong enough to know the way
and made strong enough to follow and to lead.
Made strong enough to bleed out if that is what's necessary.

We are made strong that we might lend strength.

Made strong to stride beside our kin for a mile
or two.
Made strong to be still.
Made strong to do.
Made strong to be what we will.

We are made strong to believe
and leave behind what we don't.

Listen: We are made strong.
Feel it in the mind
in the bones
in the guts
in the heart
in the spirit.
We are made strong.

On Trying

Do or do not; there is no try. —Yoda

Just a word false.
An empty ideal, trying.
Trying to love;
do love
or do not love.

And what would a
Jedi Master say
about love?

Love unrequited
altered could be with
Jedi mind tricks
but that leading down
the path to the Dark Side.

I say this:
Do love.

Threads

Every moment somewhere
        there's a dawn original and provocative
lusty and hot-blooded
a day's beginning unweighed; its treasure's worth
measured in the spending of human endeavour.

What we do together is creation:
        the celebration of existence.
Bliss is meant to be a permanent state of being,
a way of seeing divinity in the moment.
In this moment we are made,
made for singing madly
        made for moving mountains
                made for laughing
                        made for having potential realized
made to be healers and seers
        made obviously to be believers.
We are weavers of threads:
threads of colors
threads of words
threads of visions to move us towards a collective consciousness
without divisions.

We might see this in a thousand years
            or more, or less;
we'll all be here still, and still blessed.

A Line I Can't Find a Poem For

The dream is dreaming itself.
—Kalahari Bushmen saying

rough cut lines of perception

The Poem For the Line

the drummers drumming
in the jungle,
the ceaseless line of surf sounds,
an orange sari
wrapped around the line;
these are all precious
imprints
creating the
          rough cut lines of perception.

Imagination
for Chris Westray

furious imagination
leads thoughts into
the mind wilderness like
rain falling on wildebeests
running startled and mad
towards cliffs and leaping off
and growing wings and then flying
toward the sun and the sun
burning the feathers and
parachutes opening carrying
them placid into
raging waters running rough
narrow and ragged
all across the grasslands
from the very peaks of mountains
eventually wearing them down
and disappearing
into the ocean
and getting
lost in ocean salt water and evaporating
and forming snow clouds and falling
now into cool mountains calm
and snow white and blank carrying the prodigal, procreant urge
of all imagination.

NATURE

Nature

A sleeping cicada sleeping on the wall.
A lizard looking spies the sleeping cicada:
run
jump twist
 down the wall
one lick
    crunch.
I could see the wings
 trying to fly
out of the lizard mouth
legs, trying to crawl,
another crunch,
a gulp:
gone.

The lizard's sides pulse.

Impossible to Tell

Flying west from Mumbai
towards London-town,
there,
at a certain height,
in a certain light,
it is impossible to tell
the difference
between the sea and the sky,
both being an inseparable
slate gray with cornflower blue
and turned or transformed or merged
or reunited or maybe
just recognized as
being the same.

Cloudy Day

Ah, field of sunflowers
all looking west:
Have you worshipped in vain today?

The sun's not been seen
        and but hardly felt.
How do you feel
looking at clouds?

Grass

I've come to know that
it can be exciting watching
the grass grow up to my
knees. Spring rains
and it's May and the grass
covers my feet, tickles my
calves; neighbors surely
think us lazy, this naturalizing
of our yard.
Dandelions have reached epic
heights here and those little
white flowers have stems
a foot and a half tall;
a thing of beauty I say.

The landlord is here now though
with his mower and
the harshness of blades
and I can't stay here
smoking cigarettes on the porch
while the yard is murdered.

Grass

Juliet's Garden

Constant order I see:
every seed sown
becomes a plant known
by colour, by smell
by touch and by taste.

Each day's turn
brings another day's sun to burn.
Did you know that Mother
Earth spins faster
the closer she gets
to the sun?

Assuring us that each new day comes
        some new thing
like a fresh bloom
and room for expansion
and each wilted stem reminds us
that all us pay the ransom
for the future
with the days of the past.

That leaves us with this day, every day.

Some flowers, they wilt
while some flowers they bloom.
Nature?
She lives on the edge of doom,
        yearning in rain
        bursting in light
awake in the day and awake in the night.

I have come to see
these mist laden dawn hills.
I have come to feel
the mid-day burn.
I have come to see
the sky spill.
I have come to all of this while learning
and learning to be still.

Little Squirrel Slim

Lookie there at Little Squirrel Slim,
runnin' on a limb,
gatherin' together food
for the family and him to eat;
when the splinter of cold hunger pierces
the gut, it's good to have a collection of nuts.

And busy, busy
his long-tailed Lizzy.
She keeps the food all hid,
savin' it for the hungry kids.

You see Slim there and you
see Slim there.
See Slim run. He has no fear
of fallin' relyin' on the force
of his natural powers.

Slim, knowing the hours
are few knows naturally what to do
before winter cold cuts clean
through his fur coat.

At night, in the tree den,
Lizzy looks at Slim and gets
dizzy for him. They get busy
in the dim light.

Lookie there at Little Squirrel Slim
runnin' on a limb.

Wildflower Haiku

I feel a sorrow:
who I am to pick wild-
flowers? To destroy

such evident song
as I see bursting forth loudly, louder than sound;

Loathing the fury
of snapped stalk between fingers
the crispness of death;

My greater sorrow:
missing you. Wildflowers I
have destroyed for you.

Pressed Wildflowers

One never knows
just how pressed
wildflowers will turn
out – turning fading
yellow pollen ground into
the pages of my portable
Beat reader –

a little prayer: don't fade on me.

Pressed Wildflowers

In Defense of Poesy Flowers

As it is the nature of nature
      to be natural,
so it is natural to be poetic
      about nature, naturally.

So, when flowers do bloom from my poems,
think ye not, 'What a pansy'.

Kentucky Fall Sunset

Kentucky fall sun setting
on full autumn peak leaf
foliage and the orange red
trees brighter for the
sun rays cutting straight
across the horizon.

Some trees are bone bare
already – the leaves lie still
on the ground.

The dust is rising up in country
fields from corn cutting
soybean cutting; the
combine machines marching
across, through fields
and filtered sun rays growing
colder quicker day by day
and too soon these front porch
sun setting scenes will
be done. Cold sun rays
on watchless winter trees.

Who could ever include all the people that have made an impact on my poetic journey? My parents, of course. They never even thought of telling me that I couldn't study creative writing and literature.

After my parents, though, we'll have to stick to those folks who've had an influence poetically. There's Mrs Cole who first awakened my poetic spirit when I was ten years old with her reading of The Highwayman by Alfred Noyes. Then there's Professor Anne Neelon from my alma mater, Murray State University, who kindly and gently taught us the ins and outs of verse; telling us not to worry about meter, that one day we'd just hear it.

My good friend BJ Wilson: the first 'poet' I'd ever met; in the 3rd floor lobby he'd say his poems, having my full attention. Dan Dietrich, BJ Wilson, and I would spend some long afternoons and nights reading poetry, discussing poetry, taking poetry classes together, and writing poetry together. Kindred spirits we were; our own self-contained poetry movement in a little town in western Kentucky. Moving abroad, in South Korea, there was Duane Vorhees and The Seoul Artists' Network (SAN). The SAN open mic, held in Woodstock, a GI rock and roll bar, was a great place to cut my performing teeth. (Thanks to the owner, Mr. Wu, for all the whiskey; it was a help.) Duane Vorhees is still one of my favorite poets, a valuable critic, and a good friend. This book of poems was greatly enhanced by the editing work of poet and friend El Presidente Keith Francese, who along with Duane and myself, was a one-time president of the SAN. And now I'd like to thank those folks in Britain who've put me up in front of people to say some poems: Andi Langford-Woods and the Acoustic Night crew, Pete Hogg and The Wandering Word family, Antonia Bowen-Jones for giving me The Arts House Open Mic, and then there's the city of Bristol itself for being a hot-bed of poetic talent and wonderful nights. And Clive Birnie for making poetry books. Most importantly, I'd like to thank Rebecca Cant, my wife, for always listening to my poems and for being the inspiration for a good few of them; and she did the illustrations.

Without these aforementioned wonderful individuals and institutions, I might not even be a poet and certainly not the poet who wrote these poems. I also thank you if you are holding this book in your hands (unless you stole it, but even that would be okay because that means you really wanted my words). And I think that pretty much covers it.